RU Screw

101 Things Wrong with Rutgers

By G.S. Luthra

Cover design by G.S. Luthra

www.gsluthracreations.com

eBook ISBN: 978-0-9997960-6-1

Paperback ISBN: 978-0-9997960-4-7

Contents

New 2019 Foreword

I Know What You're Thinking

Why I Wrote this Book...2

Why I made the Grave Mistake of Going to this School...2

What was it like going there................................4

Why the Hell did I go to this Place?.........................5

What the Student Body is Like...........................6

The RU Screw is Real.......................................7

How it Affected me...8

How Rutgers LIED to me and Screwed me over Costing me over $10k!...9

Why God, Why?..10

Common Myths about Rutgers Dispelled..............10

101 Things Wrong with Rutgers

$300 Parking Fee...13

They don't give a 100% Refund if you Drop a Course...14

Faculty Fails to Show Up for Appointments............15

You Can't Go Anywhere without Taking the Dame Bus...15

Completely Incompetent Administration...............17

No Sleep...18

Excessive Workload...18

Drug Problem on Campus...................................19

You Will Learn Nothing......................................20

Discrimination of American Students...................21

They Favor Immigrants and Minorities Over Americans..21

Long Commute...22

It's all a Big Hype..23

Princeton Rejects...23

Not as Friendly as You'd Think...........................24

Retarded Testing Rules.....................................24

Painful Metal Seats...25

Parking is Atrocious..25

They Can Kick You Out of Your Courses for No Reason...26

Stupid College Kids..27

Scarce Opportunities..28

You're on Your Own..29

Dirty Bathrooms...30

Unprofessional Professors..................................32

Terrible TAs..32

Academic Snobs...34

Cutthroat Competition..35

Darkness Eludes the Skies................................36

It's Ridiculously Left-wing..................................37

Smelly College Kids..38

Depression and Suicide are Rampant.................39

It is Very Expensive..43

The Campus Feels Like a Third World................43

Bums on the Bus...44

It's in the S**t-Hole City of New Brunswick...........44

Horrible Bus System...50

REALLY BAD Professors who CAN'T TEACH for a
Can of Beans..50

Too Much Diversity...52

Chaotic Lectures...53

Attendance is Taken on Your Phone...................53

Recitation..54

Online Recitation..55

It's Overcrowded..56

The Campus Mimics a City..................................56

There's Crime Every Week..................................57

Scam Apartments Take Advantage of Students......58

Registering for Classes Sucks............................62

You have to Pay to Join a Club............................62

No Time for Leisure...63

Super Liberal Campus.......................................64

False Rape Culture..66

You Can't Do Real Research...............................66

Cocky City Dwellers..67

Street Bums...67

STDs are Everywhere..68

Dirty Dorms...68

Rutgers Hides Millions in Offshore Bank Accounts..69

Campus is Too Big..69

Really Bad Tutors Who Don't Give a S**t.............70

Girls Get Special Treatment...............................71

Classes are a Big Waste of Time........................71

Cheating is Mandatory for Survival......................72

Rigged Reputation..73

Labs are Taught by Grad Students, NOT Professors...74

It's a Soulless Place...75

Political Correctness...75

Hub for Migrants...75

Too Many Immigrants...76

Rigged Admissions...77

It's High School Part 2...78

Stupid Sign Holders, Religious Nuts, and Preachers...79

They Allow People on Campus Who Shouldn't be there...80

Dating Scene Sucks...81

Loneliness...82

Social Justice Warriors are Running the Place.......82

Women Blame Men for "Toxic Masculinity"............85

The President of the School DOES NOT Want to Lower Tuition...87

Transferring Courses is a Pain...88

Student Success is Exaggerated...88

Dominated by Big Pharma...89

Student Protests...89

Professors Like Failing You...90

Their Facilities are a Joke...............................91

Not Respected...91

The Weekend Bus Schedule Sucks....................92

Libraries are Packed......................................93

Subpar Education..93

Online Homework..94

Lack of Course Availability.............................95

Cafeteria..95

Electronic Participation Devices.....................96

Student Legal Services..................................96

Bad Food..98

Rude Bus Drivers...99

Silly City and School Events.........................100

Unpleasant Atmosphere...............................101

Nobody Knows What They're Doing.................101

You See the Same People.............................102

Really Old Campus Buildings.........................102

Elitism..103

Rutgers Might Shut Down..............................104

The Verdict: THIS SCHOOL SUCKS!

Better Alternatives to Stinky Rutgers and Yes, I Hope this Lowers their Enrollment...............................107

Save yourself from Getting Screwed...................108

Student's Review Reveals All...........................109

Where am I now?

How I Did at other Schools..............................111

RU Student? My Frank Advice to You................112

2019 Update...113

FREE College!...115

What if You Have to Go to Rutgers?.....................116

New 2019 Foreword

I revised this book because I wrote it out of anger which you'll soon understand why. While I have kept the original content intact, I made some slight edits to improve readability. To be clear, I'm not saying no one should go to Rutgers at all. However, I do strongly recommend against it without having done two years at community college. I've met a lot of bright students who were unsure of where to go for higher education. Many have been brainwashed into believing big name schools are the only answer and that if they go elsewhere, they won't get the same opportunities. Understand these are just illusions created by university marketers to trick you into going to their school (so they make money). Rutgers's so called "rigorous" coursework is nothing more than cheap mass-produced online education. Having one professor teach 500 students in a class is ridiculous and this has created a breed of cold faculty who couldn't care less. Learning becomes a self-responsibility, and one does not need to pay thousands of dollars for that. With that kind of money, you are better off going to community college and save yourself the trouble. It matters not which school you go to, but rather what you make of it. The education I earned at Stockton University was a thousand times better than Rutgers because I took control of my learning and their curriculum better suited my needs.

Don't go to the best ranked school, go to the school that is best for you. Too many naively think that they must go to the bigger schools, that somehow smaller ones are inferior, but this is false. The plague of consumer culture has infected America as most millennials think bigger is better. I've seen many students hesitantly choose Rutgers by default because they don't know where else to go. They don't realize that they can get the same degree at other lesser known schools. Even for fields such as engineering, Rutgers is not the only answer. In fact, Stockton has a duel degree partnership where students complete their BS in a STEM field of their choosing at Stockton while simultaneously earning a BS in their selected field of engineering. All they have to do is a couple of courses at Rowan, NJIT, or Rutgers. So you see, there are other options available and I encourage you to do more research instead of just going along with the crowd.

I've met plenty of smart kids at community and other state colleges, and most of them hated Rutgers. They complained it's dirty, old, and their poor bus system is unnecessarily frustrating. One girl told me she cried when she went there during a campus tour, so go figure. I remember even in high school, an honor roll student said that getting into Rutgers was a joke. Also, many students will tell you that the Rutgers campus has a dark eerie feeling as though it were haunted. I met a guy in my calculus class at Ocean County Community College who was thinking about transferring to Rutgers. Although, he wasn't sure, the thing he vented to me about was the $300 parking permit fee you have to pay for EACH campus. He believed that as a student, he should not have to pay $300 for every campus, it should be a one fee that allows students to park on all campuses.

Annoyances like this are among the many reasons why students need to rethink attending this school. This book is going to give you an inside look at how Rutgers and pretty much every big state university operates. They only care about increasing their profits, not about education. Certain students (usually international ones) are selected, because admin knows they will make the school's reputation look good to attract new suckers. This creates a false image, and unfortunately many believe it. This book is to help see through the illusion, so you avoid getting what is popularly known as the "RU Screw".

What is the RU Screw? Well, according to Urban Dictionary, it's –

The tendency for Rutgers University to f**k you over in some way or another due to their incompetence. Be it financially, academically, or otherwise. It eventually happens to everybody that attends the university.

Example 1: Transfer to Rutgers from another college, lose a year worth of credits. You got the RU Screw.

Example 2: Supposed to graduate in May? NOPE! Registrar f**ked up your GPA calculations and you were deleted from the graduation list. You got the RU Screw.

Example 3: Financial aid department f**ked up and your registration was canceled. You got the RU Screw.

Example 4: Buy a $300 parking permit, get to campus and there is not a single f**king parking spot available or the lot/garage is just plain closed because it's full. You got the RU Screw.

Like many, I too believed the notion that going to Rutgers was good because "there's more opportunity". The reality was such a slap in the face that I had to write this book to help others become fully informed before making the decision to attend schools like this. The good news is you can learn from my misfortune. I left the original manuscript untouched; the only additions are this new foreword and an updated section about what I did after leaving this horrendous place.

Rutgers is like a cult. The typical common response to anyone who criticizes it is "no one is going to give you a handout". The stupidity of this statement is absurd. You're PAYING FOR A SERVICE called education. If you pay $18,000 for private tennis lessons at a well-respected luxurious club and they give you third world treatment, would you have this same idiotic mentality? Of course not, you would demand a refund and warn others. Many complained about Trump University being a scam, but what about schools like

Rutgers who advertises Ivy League level education offered at an affordable price? They claim they want to remain a public institute available for everyone, but the reality is the costs, research opportunities, and job prospects are not significantly better compared to other schools. It's slick marketing. Most students are not having super success like the way admin would like you to believe. I've even seen "small class sizes" advertised on the Rutgers website, which is a complete lie, so when a school like this blatantly misleads people, how come no one gets angry? Well I' am, because I got screwed, and want to warn everyone about the false promises and expectations about this joke of a school. So consider this book my warning to you to refrain from going to Rutgers. You, the student, are paying for quality education in a first world nation, so you should expect the best in the world but what you get at Rutgers resembles that of a third world nation like India.

Students need to be pickier about their education, and demand perfection just like consumers do for high end products and services. Just like how many low informed people believe that moving to the city is going to somehow magically make them rich and successful, many aspiring students think that going to big schools like Rutgers will magically propel their academic career. The reality is, no, you will not make it big like the students they advertise on their website. The city is filled with massive competition with people from all over the world and Rutgers is no different. Instead of competing for jobs, you're competing for classes, tutors, and research opportunities against other students, many of whom have had better academic training. Such an environment does not breed learning but rather competition, elitism, and degeneracy. That's why many students become alcoholics, potheads, and drug addicts. Those that eventually do get a stable career unfortunately carry these bad habits with them. Sadly, there are those who take their own life, and the school is very good at keeping the real suicide numbers hush, hush.

Read this book with an open mind and don't let the strong language get to you. After all, I did get RU screwed, costing me over $10k, so it's normal to be angry.

Enjoy the read

- G.S. Luthra

I Know What You're Thinking

This guy is a loser who is whining and complaining about not making it, that's what you're thinking right? Believe me I knew what the risks were of publishing this book and what it would do to me, but the atrocious so-called education was so bad at Rutgers that it had to be written, because nobody is saying anything due to fear. This school is like a cult, and believe me, I' am speaking for many through this book.

I've met plenty who hated this school and I can tell you that there are many more who feel the same way. Thousands have suffered just like me but are too afraid to speak out, so this book is to warn others to avoid this school.

Colleges should be held accountable for their education because what they claim counters what they deliver.

Think of it this way, this school angered me so much, screwed me over so badly, that it prompted me to write this book, so there is a purpose to it.

Why I wrote this book

Before you write me off as some disgruntled college dropout, understand that prior to enrolling at my first and last semester at Rutgers, I held several degrees in business and design. I had already done most of my science course work like organic chemistry, and biology at my previous school and wanted to finish a degree in science.

Visit my website to see my resume and accomplishments till date, you'll see that it's more than what most college grads have done. I have done well in tough subjects like chemistry, mathematics, and physics. You can lash out all kinds of opinions, but if you are intelligent, you will conclude that there is a reason why I wrote this book.

Why I made the Grave Mistake of Going to this School

At the time, I thought that it would be better to go as Rutgers had the most graduate programs. I was also sick and tired of going to the same college for the past ten years. I felt that I wasn't getting anywhere and believed going to a bigger school would change everything with new opportunities. I felt embarrassed and ashamed that I still hadn't gotten anywhere so thought a different school was the solution.

My uncles had been pushing me to go to Rutgers in the past, because I had cousins who went there and did very well financially. In their mind, they believed that my lack of success was due to the school I was going to which I agreed at the time, but they thought that by going to Rutgers, everything would work out well. Additionally, one of my uncles offered financial assistance which was a big factor in my decision. I was in between continuing at Stockton or taking a chance at Rutgers.

When I visited the Rutgers campus with my uncle, he was surprised because it was a total dump as you'll soon learn more about, and when he saw Stockton's campus, he then instead recommended continuing there, so I went home to think about it. I had been listening to the glories of Rutgers for so long, and now suddenly Stockton was okay. But then at the last minute, I got a call at night from my other uncle whose long boring lecture finally convinced me to transfer to Rutgers as I had heard enough. I just wanted out, away from Stockton and my monotonous life. I thought my luck would change at Rutgers. There were other reasons like not being able to get a suitable apartment near Stockton, and no other available housing options.

Basically, I went there because I was tired of commuting to Stockton University for ten years, my original school, and had enough of the negative atmosphere at home. Going to Rutgers was more of an escape if anything, because it was the only practically way I could get out of my negative environment since I didn't have the financing to move out on my own.

As you'll soon learn, that was a very bad decision…

What it was like going there

In a nutshell, it was hell. I really wish I never went there, and I questioned why God allowed me to go when I begged him to help guide me to make the right decision. Perhaps he wanted me to warn you and many other future students, so I hope this sheds some light on your quest for higher education.

Why the Hell did I Go to This Place?

You might be wondering, why would I even go to this dump in the first place? It was because it was the fastest option to escape the negative atmosphere at home, and I thought Rutgers would enhance my academic pursuits. Luck wasn't on my side at the time, at least not in finances and my home situation was unbearable, so I took the exit. That was really the number one reason, I just couldn't stand living there with everything falling apart, and I just couldn't take it any longer.

My uncle understood my situation, so he offered financial assistance which I accepted as I was at the point where I saw no other option. I knew I wasn't going to make enough money quick enough to get out of there, so I took it even though I didn't want to.

What the Student Body is Like

Walking around the huge campus, hopping from bus to bus, I noticed a few immediate things about the student body:

- Races tend to stick with themselves
- F**k you, that's the overall vibe on campus
- Everyone is overly stressed

It seems that whatever they were told about this school was a lie and the shock has put them in a permanent depression mode, at least until they graduate, that is if they ever do.

The RU Screw is Real

All the horrors you've heard about it are true. This school is a big rip off, I'm surprised at how in the world they get away with it on a regular basis. Year after year, this school robs innocent students of their money and I'm certain there are government payoffs to keep it under the rug, because it is common knowledge for all students that this school takes advantage of them, yet nobody dares say a word. It's almost as if it were a cult where students are too scared to utter one negative word about Rutgers else, they'll be crucified by peers, but I know they are there, because I've met them, and it shocked the heck out of me.

Student after student vented to me about how much they hated Rutgers, and how badly it screwed them over. They had nowhere else to go and wish they never attended. I know many schools can be a drag, but Rutgers is on a whole new level. The good things you might have heard are overhyped. It may have been good long ago but it's nothing like what it used to be. Their reputation is pathetic. Ask anyone who knows on the inside (like me), and they'll tell you the truth.

This school should be shut down immediately.

How it Affected me

It was easily one of the worst experiences of my life. I lost a whole semester and wasted thousands of dollars. The stress created urges in me like never before. I wanted alcohol, sex, just something to take away the pain of daily life. Sticking to a healthy vegetarian diet was not feasible so I broke my seven-year streak and ate meat, and a lot of junk food.

It still hurts me deeply when thinking about it, and how my family's money was wasted. It is injustice and I pray God makes them pay for all the thousands of students they screw on a regular basis.

How Rutgers Lied and Screwed Me Over Costing me over $10k!

Prior to enrolling, I had contacted their science department to confirm whether there were prospects of doing the research that I had expressed. I never got a clear answer, instead a lot of transferring to different professors but eventually I was given some hope so long as the grades are right, and I could find a willing professor. I was given the impression that most, if not all, of my previous courses would be transferred and that it would not take long for me to complete the degree, do research, and continue onto grad school.

Housing there is overly priced and limited so I had to find a place on my own nearby and the prices there for a decent livable place were atrocious. Sure, you can find a cheaper rent, that is if you want to share a shack with hooligans that any gangbanger can kick the door open, but if you want a place that's safe for normal people, you must pay top dollar just like you would to live on campus at Rutgers. The benefit of living on your own, is that you don't have to put up with roommates and you become more responsible looking after yourself.

Why God, why?

This was the question I kept asking over and over again, even after I left. The pain I suffered was just not fair and I didn't do anything in life to deserve such injustice. I don't want to make up some answer that it was somehow part of a divine plan. I will just say that I was misled and scammed into going there and got the infamous "RU Screw".

Common Myths about Rutgers Dispelled

I was told many things by older folks about Rutgers, however what they said was very outdated. There are many false perceptions students are given and when they finally do attend Rutgers, they are shocked by the reality. So, here are some misconceptions people have about it:

You meet new people – wrong, once you get into the groove, you end up seeing the same people, because in the city you're stuck doing the same routine

There's endless opportunity – it's just another sales pitch. Professors are arrogant and look down on you. They lured me in with the hope of promising research, but I say stay away, the only opportunity you get is to be your professor's lapdog and assist with THEIR research, not yours

Great qualified professors – WHAT, are you freaking kidding me? For physics lab, I had a graduate student from China as the teacher. He didn't speak English nor taught the material clearly. My calculus professor ignored me for some reason and my genetics professor had this cold dark aura about him. Looking into his eyes, it felt like talking to a grey alien. My chemistry professor was nice, but the class was just way too big and student shenanigans made it near impossible to learn

Like you, I believed in the concept that going to a bigger big-name school like Rutgers is better for your academic pursuits, because there are supposedly more opportunities. The truth, however, is that this is a clever marketing ploy used to reel in students. Theoretically, yes, there are more options but having more variety isn't always a good thing. It's better to have a few things done right than a plethora of chaos. Unfortunately, this lie of

11

bigger is better has infected the minds of students and as a result, everyone holds onto the concept that big state schools are better. After attending Rutgers, I developed a greater appreciation for Stockton. It is far superior academically, and better in every aspect. The research I did there was great, but because I had this false image of Rutgers, I went there when I shouldn't have. The good news is I've noticed more students waking up to the fallacy of big-name and even Ivy League schools, because the hefty price tag isn't worth the stress and headache. College should be about learning, not competing, and education requires a personal approach, not blasting out cheaply produced mass online education. This is what schools like Rutgers do, and you need to be aware.

Visiting the school itself will give more insight and it is recommended before making the commitment as with everything else. And now without further delay, here are 101 things wrong with Rutgers -

101 Things Wrong with Rutgers

Here it is, the infamous list of why you should stay clear of this place at all costs. Not only will your academic performance be saved, but so will your sanity:

1. $300 Parking Fee

WTF? That was my first reaction when I learned that I had to pay this amount just to be able to park on campus as a commuter!

Yup, that's right. Just to park on campus to go to class requires you to purchase a very expensive permit. It doesn't even come with a goodie bag, just some crappy sticker paper that looks like it's from the gutter. Yes, you are getting screwed. The sooner you realize it, the faster you'll transfer out to greener pastures.

You'll never see this at other smaller schools and that's why I advocate them, even medium sized schools are better.

Stockton University used to give free parking passes, and now recently they dealt away with it and have an automated system where you just register your vehicle and viola, you're golden! Rutgers, however, prefers to milk students for every last bogus charge they can get out of them. Real caring, aren't they?

2. They don't give a 100% Refund if you Drop a Course

I was shocked to find out that on the first day of class, you lose your ability get your money back if you have to leave for some reason.

I've been to many schools and they all have similar policies of giving students a good week to add or drop courses without losing money. If you were to drop during this grace period, you get 100% refund, but Rutgers doesn't, because they're greedy money snatchers. Once it starts, you're stuck. Other schools at least give you a couple days to get your money back, however I'm seeing this trend spreading everywhere.

3. Faculty Fails to Show Up for Appointments

Many students have told me that even after going through hell to schedule an appointment whether with professors or administrators, they would never show up due to some bulls**t reason and they would have to reschedule again.

Personally, I experienced this with tutoring. As a student, you are allowed to make a few one on one sessions with tutors, so after I scheduled a few sessions, the tutor would text me at the last minute saying that he/she can't come. Out of the several scheduled appointments I made, I only remember seeing one.

It is amazing how faculty can't even do this one simple little thing. Ridiculous.

4. You Can't Go Anywhere without Taking the Dame Bus

Walking is a risk as thugs are waiting at night, but even in the day, the campus is so stretched out that you cannot go anywhere.

You are completely dependent on the bus schedule and waiting sucks big time. It's overcrowded and many times you must wait for the next bus because it's always jam packed, making you late for class.

You will lose precious time waiting when you could be studying, resting, or doing a thousand other more productive things. You are at the mercy of the bus system as you can't go anywhere without it. Walking is pointless and dangerous as crime is rampant in in the city.

At other normal colleges, students can freely walk to classes and enjoy the beauty of their campus, but not at Rutgers. It's always a rush hopping on this bus to get to that bus to arrive at this station just so you can catch another ride to another campus.

The school is just too dame big for its own good and getting around is a hassle. It's also dangerous when you have late afternoon or night classes because you'll end up getting back home late at night. I remember walking on the city streets around 11:30 P.M. to get home on multiple occasions because that's what happens. The bus is late, it's jam-packed, you get stuck on campus, etc., so it's not uncommon to arrive home late and exhausted.

5. Completely Incompetent Administration

I really feel bad for students there. The people whom you need to help you with class registration and what not, are unqualified, and for lack of better word, dumb. Whenever you need help, they always reply with "that's not my department". They like to claim that this mistreatment trains you for the real world, but even if you go to a gas station or a bar for directions, or even to a homeless person, you'll get more help than Rutgers admin.

You'll hear a lot of "You can't do that", by squeaky voiced admin, and scripted answers as if you pressed a button to hear a pre-recorded message.

For some reason, staff and admin have a chip on their shoulder as if Rutgers were Ivy League, so they give you an attitude for nothing.

6. No Sleep

Due to the hectic soul draining city lifestyle, I couldn't sleep even if I did everything right and went to bed early. There was just something off. I would be up till 2am and wake up at 7. It's fine if you've got a job to do for a while, but if you do it every day it takes a serious toll on your health.

7. Excessive Workload

Professors dump piles of assignments while the school encourages you to join clubs and "network". How is that feasible when you must study all the time? Mass produced education isn't working for them. Rutgers thinks that by dumping meaningless online homework like WebAssign, (which sucks by the way, because it is nothing like the exams) and making tests unnecessarily harder than they already are, they are somehow making their programs more "rigorous". It drives students crazy, causing them to become suicidal, and they are not learning anything. The workload is ridiculous as they're competing with Ivy League schools.

A good example is the ACS chemistry test being more direct and less confusing compared to Rutgers exams. One dumb a$$ calculus professor of mine kept saying Rutgers has one of the best math programs in the world, but snickers and sneers filled the classroom as students knew they were learning nothing from him, nor was it one of the "best math programs" in the nation.

"Statistics" like these are very easily rigged to make schools look appealing to potential suckers, I mean students. Everyone wants to die due to the workload; you can see it on their faces of depression. You see it on the buses, on the streets, it's everywhere…and it's terrible. Ask anybody enrolled there and they'll tell you that it's all just a big waste of time and money.

Administration does it because online work allows them to cut costs and keep more profits. Greedy scumbags…

8. Drug Problem on Campus

Despite the known negative effects of marijuana, students smoke it like it's the end of the world. I knew a guy who worked security at these parties and described one where the house was stuffed with Rutgers students and crack was being passed around like candy.

Surprisingly, most of the users according to him were Indians since the place was packed with them.

9. You Will Learn Nothing

Life becomes very mechanical with the sole focus being grades, not education. I was very surprised to hear from engineering students who were about to graduate admit to me that they felt scared and unprepared because they lacked confidence in their abilities. They told me that they learned nothing.

One Chinese guy told me that he doesn't know what he's doing, because coding as he said was like talking to an alien race. Most kids just do whatever it takes to do well on tests, while not actually learning anything. Don't take my word for it, go and ask students yourself.

10. Discrimination of American Students

International students are cruising, because they're fully funded with all their expenses are paid. They had better training in high school in their homeland and outperform American students, because the education is so bad in the U.S. that students are not prepared well, and they ultimately suffer.

Professors are imported from third world countries and they give students a hard time unnecessarily. You don't have teachers; you have academics who couldn't care less about students' success.

11. They Favor Immigrants and Minorities Over Americans

Mexican, and other Hispanics are given preference while the American student waits in the back of the line for everything – funding, service, opportunity, etc. Nobody says anything, but it is clearly apparent.

Blacks are cruising, they get special treatment as repayment for what the "evil white man" did to them. International students and minorities get more opportunities as this excessive diversity is killing the American citizen student.

12. Long Commutes

Because of the stretched-out campus of Rutgers, commuting takes a long time whether by bus or car. Parking on campus is a drag because you're most likely going to have to park all the way in the back due to the crowd, so you will spend a lot of time walking from the parking lot to campus, then to whatever building you're going to.

The other thing is if you only have a parking permit for one campus and you're commuting at some distance, you will lose more time because you have to park at your designated campus, then hop on board the shuttle bus to get to the actual campus that you need to get to, and then you will need to walk a lengthy distance to physically get inside your destination.

So whether you commute or use public transportation, you will lose a lot of time unnecessarily solely because of the poor structure of Rutgers.

13. It's all a Big Hype

I now have firsthand experience at a "big name" university and I must say, I'm very disappointed. All schools whether Ivy League or not, glorify students who do very well while hiding the fact that most do just ok, but still have a big debt to pay off. I've seen a woman who graduated Rutgers with a degree in science working at an apartment building and know many other examples of graduates just working typical jobs, nothing special, nothing worth the debt and headache.

Never mind the few who did well that are advertised on the school's website, pay attention to the thousands and thousands of graduates who work menial jobs, that is if they one at all.

14. Princeton Rejects

I'm not sure why or where they get the arrogance from, but there are a lot of preppy freshman who just graduated high school with perfect scores and think they are a genius.

My suspicion is that they are Princeton rejects who think they're better than everyone else and look down on them thinking they're big s**t. Everyone has a chip on their shoulder which makes no sense because it's not like they're in Harvard or Princeton.

15. Not as Friendly as You'd Think

I was expecting everyone to be a lot friendlier, but no, everyone saw each other as a competitor and people stuck to their own kind – Blacks hung out with the brothas, Asian gangs, Indians, etc. For a school that shouts diversity, it's amazing at how easily own can feel isolated.

16. Retarded Testing Rules

You will be required to make the trip to Rutgers late at night or on the weekend where you will be given a preassigned seat that you'll have to find in a giant room filled with over a hundred students all scampering around doing the same thing. While you are taking the test, idiot skinny soy boy facilitators will walk around acting like they're CIA who will demand for your identification while you're taking a difficult test. I wanted to sock them. The tests also read like they were created by the dorkiest beta males, probably while masturbating in their underwear.

17. Painful Metal Seats

Also, the seats are very small so if you're over six feet tall, you're going to be uncomfortable the entire time. The university is old, and the seats were made for a time when the height and weight averages were much lower.

Taking tests are the worst, because you're trying to solve difficult problems yet can't find a good position in the metal fused seats. I often heard girls complaining that their butts wore sore after tests. A good ole' fashion spanking would have taken care of it.

18. Parking is Atrocious

As if the fee was enough insult, finding an open spot is like playing the lottery, sometimes you win but most times you lose.

And if you make the mistake of parking somewhere where you are not supposed to, expect to be slapped with fees. I've heard girls venting that they had to pay parking tickets in the amount of $375.

19. They Can Kick You Out of Your Courses for No Reason

System glitches are not uncommon, and a lot of students have fallen victim to it where they were kicked out just like that. One day, I woke up in the middle of the semester and found that I had been withdrawn from the school. I freaked out and had to call admin for help to get me back in and of course got transferred to multiple departments to finally speak to someone who knew what they were doing. It took the whole day, and then multiple days waiting from them to fix it and the stress drove me crazy. I thought I was out.

As if the stress of classes wasn't already bad enough, I had to deal with this rubbish and I'm not the only one whose had this sort of an issue. Tales like this are common among the student body.

Like I said, this school is too big for its own good. It cannot manage it properly and students are the ones who suffer. They seriously need to downgrade to a more manageable size.

20. Stupid College Kids

They're easily the dumbest student body I've ever seen. I never met one intelligent soul. There was one Black kid in my chemistry class who had the maturity level of a retarded child. This guy sang metrosexual pop in class and to the professor when she walked in. Maybe I'm just old fashion, but is this normal in a university classroom? I can understand in kindergarten, but this is not appropriate at a university.

This Black kid liked to hop around class like a monkey and would laugh like Dr. Jekyll. Of course, he got away with it since everyone is afraid of being called a racist. There many antics that occur on campus and surrounding areas because college idiots get drunk and end up doing really dumb s**t.

21. Scarce Opportunities

Colleges are good at marketing their star students, and Rutgers is no exception. When Ivy League schools show you all the billionaires who dropped out of their school, they are subliminally making you think that if only you could just attend their institution, you will be set for life. All your financial problems will be automatically taken care of. Wrong, this trend is seen everywhere but is adjusted according the ranking and prestige of the university for effective marketing campaigns. Rutgers is big on research and showcases their stellar students doing hyped up groundbreaking research that is propagandized to sway you into thinking that you too will have a similar experience if you go there. The reality is, you are competing with nearly a hundred thousand other students and those whom you see being advertised had already been preselected beforehand. Let me explain.

Rutgers like other universities, tactfully admits prodigy students who they know will do well, particularly from foreign nations like India and China because they can be easily controlled. Of course, they are also promoting minorities, specifically Blacks and Hispanics for the same reason just to throw you a bone and make the school look good, politically that is. I don't care about the few anomalies that you may have seen, I care about the statistics of graduates and the numbers show that they aren't doing any better than those who go to other smaller schools.

No, you will not be able to do the research you've been dreaming about, no, you will not get those six-figure job offers, and no, you will not be magically offered a lucrative position at a big company where you can live the fabulous life. All of that is part of a sales pitch designed to make you want to attend their university.

Rutgers, like all government funded schools, are good at showing you flashy ads to give you the illusion that you'll make it big at their school. Don't be fooled.

22. You're on your Own

It begs repeating. Nobody cares about you and you'll have to deal with your problems all by yourself. The student mentors, advisors, and tutors assigned to you don't give a dame. Don't believe me, go see for yourself and blow thousands of dollars on fourth-world education.

23. Dirty Bathrooms

What does a guy have to do for a paper towel? Restrooms are disgusting and even with all this government money, they can't pay someone to keep a full stock of paper towels. In addition to that, there's graffiti everywhere.

For example, take this one that I saw at Busch campus –

In case you can't read it, it says,

"I don't always engage in bestiality, but when I do I prefer horse cock."

"Stay stallion hungry my friends."

That's what you get at Rutgers.

24. Unprofessional Professors

My calculus professor had his "office hours" at a small round table at a pizza cafe. I had trouble comprehending it because I thought office hours meant at an actual office like any other student would. When I finally found him, he looked away not even acknowledging me, and even after I followed him and sat at his "office", he didn't seem to want to help anybody. All he did was just bulls**t with students.

That's all professors want to do, they just want to tell jokes, run home, and do nothing. Such people should not be in these positions.

25. Terrible TAs

When taking a class, if you've never seen the material before, you need to be taught how to get to the solution, but these teacher's assistants don't want to help you get answers. They expect you to just know it, and they're bad teachers themselves.

In physics lab, I never saw my professor, instead I had these Chinese TA who was virtually useless. His favorite line was "I don't want to give you the answer, but that's incorrect." He also sent us emails telling that he'll punish us if we use incorrect formulas. That's the kind of third-world communist treatment that you'll have to deal with. Not worth paying $20,000.

Go to a smaller no-name school, you'll get better education.

They expect you to find the answer, but if you've never seen the material before, how can you find it? You can spend all day, but if you don't know, you'll just be going around in circles. It's like telling you a phrase in German and then giving you a book to read in German and write a paper on it. Even with the internet, it will take you the whole day or longer to figure it out, not something full-time college kids can afford to do.

Be prepared to teach yourself everything. I remember studying a calculus book that I got from a local county library on the floor (had no furniture at my apartment). That was my dedication even though Rutgers's library didn't have one decent book on math.

Community college is so much better. Ask any student and they'll all tell you how much better it is to take classes, particularly in STEM, at community college compared to Rutgers.

26. Academic Snobs

The student body consists of spoiled pretentious over privileged brats that had everything handed to them in life. It's something you would expect to see at Princeton, but these guys have their heads way over inflated. It's worse with the professors as they act like they're gods with their pet student assistants who treat you like crap.

If you dare question them, you're asking for trouble. I've met some who have, but it doesn't take you anywhere because the college ultimately has the power over your grades.

Welcome to Nazi University.

27. Cutthroat Competition

Just like in New York, you will face extreme competition. There's nothing wrong with competing, but what you get at Rutgers is not normal. The odds are against you and there's very little that you can practically do.

Everyone is seeking a job by any means necessary. Job fairs where "networking" takes place are nothing but a$$ kissing fiestas where students dress in the typical slave attire (suits and skirts) and try to impress corporate executives. You're a mouse trying to grab his bite of cheese in a cesspit of rodents all trying to snatch their share.

Diving into a competition with 60,000+ students is a fool's journey, unless you've got an edge such as family connections or other prior contacts which is often the case with those who get jobs at big companies. Being LGBT or a social justice warrior, or a liberal/socialist/communist also improves your chances too. Or just spray paint yourself to change your skin color to that of a minority. It's worked wonders for some.

28. Darkness Eludes the Skies

I read one girl's review of Rutgers on the Student's Review website, and she mentioned how the sky would always look dark as if the place were haunted. I'm not one to promote the existence of the paranormal, but in this case, I concur. There is something off about this place, like there's some sort of malevolent entity running the school.

No matter which campus you go – Bush, Douglas, Livingston, Cook, there's this eerie feeling. I guess that's why it attracts so many hooligans who love it. Bugs love living in muck and filth, so all I can say is that when you enter Rutgers, you will feel a strange presence of pure evil.

29. It is Ridiculously Left Wing

"Dump Trump" Protest

On the first day of molecular genetics class, the professor insulted the president by saying he was mentally unfit. He was giving the impression that Trump is some mad man ready to push the detonator to launch a nuclear missile at a moment's notice.

Of course, the class roared in laughter, but sensible people will realize that this is just another example of academia against Trump. He should pull government funding to this school and teach them a lesson.

You don't have to look far to realize that the whole campus is anti-Trump. There are a few supporters here and there, but they are specks compared to the herds of whack jobs who are Bernie supporting socialists. People can vote for who they want, but at Rutgers it is dangerous to voice your support for Trump.

Really shows how "diverse" Rutgers is.

30. Smelly College Kids

The bus system is a pain at Rutgers primarily because there's too many students and not enough buses. Especially at night when everyone is going home, the school is too cheap to send enough buses which delays you from getting home. Buses are packed, and worst of all, you brush up against dirty smelly kids. I remember one night this hobo-looking Caucasian guy wearing a hoody sat next to me. This guy stuck! It was so bad that I wanted to gag. With all that tuition money why can't Rutgers pay for more buses?

I don't mean to be mean nor am I picking on any one race, but I've had it with these college kids that stink, and I mean bad! I take hygiene very seriously, because being in martial arts there's an old saying, the stronger you are, the stronger you smell. I didn't want to write this, but as I type this I'm sitting in molecular genetics, an Asian kid just sat two seats away from me and dame man! Another time I was on the EE bus, and when this Indian guy passed by me as he went up to the bus driver, the stench hit me like a tidal wave. My nervous system was shocked from the paralyzing smell.

Again, I'm not being mean, nor picking on certain groups, but there just has been too many occurrences that's pushed me past the limit. Hey, I stink too after rigorous exercising, but I clean up and take of it. So, if you like sitting next to dirty punks, come to Rutgers, they all stink!

31. Depression and Suicide are Rampant

It surprised me to see so many posts on Facebook of students who took their own lives. These are young men and women in their prime and sadly many decided to end it all. I don't know what exactly their reasons were, but I can guess the stress from attending Rutgers most likely had something to do with it. I too had negative thoughts during my first and last semester at Rutgers, and while I didn't contemplate suicide, I did have strong urges to start drinking and other unhealthy behavior, so I can relate to those students because the anxiety levels were ridiculous.

During my time at Rutgers, I broke my vegetarian diet and ate a lot of junk food because the stress was just too much. This is what is happens to many students. I met a Chinese engineering major who told me that he once became fat because he was very depressed. Stories like this are not uncommon. Many kids turn to booze, drugs, partying, and sex because the environment is so sick and guess what, nobody cares. Why do you think Rutgers has a suicide help center and why do you think it's such a big problem there?

Psychiatric problems are so common that the school has a free clinic for students, but apparently, it isn't doing much for them.

Here's a screenshot from Facebook –

Lauren Scandariato ▸ **Rutgers University Class of 2020 (Official)** ···

9 hrs · New Brunswick, NJ · 🌐

Meet my friend, Irisa. She was a current student at Rutgers, walking around the same campuses and sitting in the same classrooms and same seats as all of you. She was a great student with ambition to work in the medical field. She seemingly had everything together with a bright future ahead. She tragically took her own life last week. It was a horrible shock, and no one knew anything was wrong. Sometimes the most unsuspecting people are going through the most pain.

If you get one thing out of this take the time to tell your parents that you love them... tell your friends that you are there for them.

Everyone should know there are resources available to them and people to help. Rutgers offers free counseling for students through the graduate program. You can call 848-932-7884 to make an appointment or stop by 17 Senior street M-F 9-4. You can also call the Rutgers Nj Hopeline at 855-654-6735 at any time.

The ultimate reason I am posting this is to help out Irisa's family with raising money. Irisa's family are the ones who are going through this rough time. Irisa has left behind her single mother and two sisters. She had student loans which now her mother must take on as a cosigner, on top of paying for the funeral. Her sisters have set up a go fund me at www.gofundme.com/irisaselfo to help their mother. Take the time to read what her sisters wrote. Whether you can help Irisa's family out financially or simply by sharing her gofundme, it would mean the world to her family.

RU Screw

👍 Like   💬 Comment   ↪ Share

😊😢🔄 710

View previous comments

 Leiby Laura Valdez I'm so sorry for your loss 😢🙏🙏
Like · Reply · 2 hrs

 Kevin Liu I know many people that hide their pain with happiness. I'm sorry for your loss, it's always the good people that leave earth too fast.
Like · Reply · 👍 1 · 1 hr

 Gabrielle Ann Sales So sorry to hear the loss of your friend. She looked ✕ like a beautiful girl. Stay strong and everyone who knew her 💜
Like · Reply · 14 mins

32. It is Very Expensive

Tuition might be okay for an in-state student, however when you add books, parking fees, and other living expenses, the costs become astronomical. After all, you are living in the city. Students quickly go bankrupt. The fees pile up, so expect to be broke and in deep debt by the time you graduate.

From textbooks to a slice of pizza to even a soda, this school is looting students. How they get away with this is beyond me.

33. The Campus Feels Like a Third World

When you get on the dirty bus, walk around the filthy campus, sit on the disgusting seats in ancient looking classrooms, it really does feel like you are getting ripped off. America is a first-world nation (supposedly), yet Rutgers doesn't exemplify first-world education. But don't take my word for it, go see it for yourself.

Don't say I didn't warn you.

34. Bums on the Bus

Drivers let homeless people hop onboard and you can't say anything or else you'll be called a racist. They enter the bus shabbily dressed, they smell, and ask students for money. One time, I found a bum sleeping in the backseat. Doesn't the school realize that letting these people ride the bus puts students at risk? Don't they know that bums can carry bed bugs, drugs, and germs? What a joke.

If you're a student, I advise you to avoid sitting in the backseat or any seat for that matter. Just stand, hold onto the pole, and wash your hands thoroughly after departure. Make sure to use sanitizer and supplement with vitamins to boost your immunity.

35. It's in the S**t-Hole City of New Brunswick

Slum Dog Millionaire could have been in New Brunswick, no need to go to India. This junky city looks like a third-world s**t-hole. There are bums everywhere, thugs, and low lives. Crime occurs every week, and it's noisy all night. Good luck going to sleep.

Every week I got emails from the police department reporting some student getting mugged, robbed, and alike on college property. Like I said, this school is that of a third world. Rutgers gives a horrible representation of a first-world nation, but it is an excellent example of how low America has fallen and how degenerate society has become. College kids think the purpose of life is to go to fulfill the fantasies they see on social media. Cities are like what a casino is to a gambler or a whorehouse to a pervert, it just offers gratification for fetishes.

Schools like Rutgers like to advertise that being in the city is a benefit, but nothing could be further from the truth. Cities in America are full of bums, trash, loud construction, and dirty suits and skirts walking around acting like they're big s**t. Cities are havens to the most ruthless people on earth. They'll lie to your face, cheat you, steal from you, or even assault you, and there's nothing you can do about it. Thinking that the police or university will be there for you is like jumping off a cliff thinking Superman will swoop down and rescue you.

New Brunswick stinks just like every other city in America. Here are some pictures I took to show you what it really looks like. Keep in mind, nearly all of these pictures were taken just outside apartment buildings that are dubbed as "luxurious".

The following photos were taken by G.S. Luthra

Ever since I moved there, I went to bed
between 1-3am at night due to noisy
hooligans on the streets. As you can see, the

city is clearly not the opulent fantasy that the school advertises. This city is merciless, it will eat you up and spit you out without any remorse.

36. Horrible Bus System

Their scheduling is terrible. Unless you're at College Ave, the main stop for all the buses, expect to wait a half an hour minimum. Technically, there is supposed to be a bus every fifteen minutes, but that is a joke. If you live off campus in the city, or if you're on one of the other campuses like Douglass, waiting for 40 minutes is not uncommon. AND when the bus comes, expect it to be packed. You may not even be able to get in and will then have to wait an additional 40 minutes!

37. REALLY BAD Professors who CAN'T TEACH for a Can of Beans

Saying they have bad professors is an understatement. They can't teach yet give you ridiculously hard tests. Professors really, really don't care. They're arrogant, snotty, and act like they're the greatest in the world even though they never produced a product or service for society. They're cowards who hide behind the power of academia, because that's the only place they can find work.

Most professors are imported from third-world nations and they can't speak proper English and are very bad at teaching, and I mean really, really, bad. They may be experts in their field, but teaching takes a skilled individual who can break down tough subjects into easy digestible chunks that even the layman can understand.

Foreign professors, teaching assistants, and tutors are not uncommon at Rutgers and they slam Americans with their third-world hammer. It's almost as if they seek vengeance and come here to get revenge on Americans by making their lives unnecessarily difficult. There are many tutoring ads posted all over, but you have to pay $20-50 per hour to these guys and still it's not worth the money.

38. Too Much Diversity

Whenever there's a majority of Caucasians at a federally funded school, admin goes crazy and as a result, many big state universities have a mass infestation of people of ethnic and even alien backgrounds. Rutgers is no exception; it has a huge international student population. Now, I don't mind having some diversity and I think it is a great thing however, there must be a limit on how many you can take.

Brining all these foreign students with their tuition fully paid is coming out of the pockets of American citizens, and many of these students do not speak proper English. On my first day at RU, I asked an Asian guy for information on the bus, but I couldn't understand a single word he said. Many students complain about having trouble understanding foreign professors. Their cultures are different, thus creating unnecessary problems. They bring that third world hard a$$ mentality to class and it doesn't help students in their learning.

Diversity is fine, but too much is bad just like with everything else.

39. Chaotic Lectures

Because Rutgers is so big, students suffer by attending unorderly classes. Classrooms with over a hundred students are typical and it's hard to hear the professor and pay attention because everyone is talking and goofing around. You can't see what the professor is writing on the board and no one is there to help you.

Students rush to the professor at the end and the crowd makes it difficult to get answers to your questions. Rutgers's greed knows no bounds as they let more and more people in to increase their profits.

Go to community college, where the most you'll have in your class is forty. Trust me I've taken science classes at community college and it is heaven compared to the Rutgers, the hellhole of New Jersey.

40. Attendance is Taken on Your Phone

They've implemented a new system that requires you to download an app to sign in for attendance. Many have trouble logging in due to bad Wi-Fi making you "miss" class even though you were physically there which can negatively affect your class grade.

41. Recitation

As if lecture weren't bad enough, they make you attend a recitation where you are put under a second-rate teacher different from your main professor, who most likely got kicked out of another school like mine who was kicked out Arizona State. You will struggle and do worse on the quizzes. It is retarded and doesn't help your lecture performance at all.

You'll also get the worst teachers at these recitations. In calculus recitation, a student questioned one problem marked wrong on his quiz and after examining, the teacher (who got kicked out of Arizona State) laughingly responded that he must have been drunk while grading.

42. Online Recitation

If you don't know what it is, online recitation is where you log into your account and virtually attend a recitation session just like when you join a chat session or instant messaging group on AOL (for those of you who remember).

This was new to me, and I hated every bit of it. You're in the chatroom where you see a small box with a live feed of your professor who then attempts to go over and teach you course material. You are required to answer annoying questions during the hour-long online recitation and that counts as part of your grade. However, if you don't answer a certain amount of questions correctly, you will have to attend another recitation again and answer the quiz questions right or else you get a zero! It's a stupid ridiculous requirement and the whole thing is just a complete waste of time because nobody learns anything. Kids goof off, insult each other, and you can't get your questions answered because there's too many people. You will not learn anything, believe me.

Go to a real school where you actually physically sit down in a lecture and have a professor who knows what they're doing.

Do not go to Rutgers, or at least do not take your science course there, take them at community college.

43. It's Overcrowded

The student population exceeds 60,000! There're way too many people there, and the university cannot accommodate it. They don't know what they're doing because they've grown way out of proportion, bigger than they can handle. And it shows, you're literally a street rat squirming around like a fish in the big sea. Like I said, Rutgers is too big for its own good. Do yourself a favor and ditch that dump!

44. The Campus Mimics a City

You may think it is good preparation for working in the city, however if you're smart, you'll know that working in the city is a bad, bad idea. Try it, and you'll see for yourself, but don't say I didn't tell you so. And don't listen to these scumbag idiots who tell you that "oh, it's like the real world, it's toughening you up, if you can make it there you can make it anywhere".

Wrong, the numbers prove otherwise. Thousands of students graduate every year from Rutgers, do you really think every single one of them are getting high paying jobs? No, most are doing stupid deskwork, or other mundane jobs working for rich people smarter than them. These positions don't require degrees, which is what I've seen graduates end up in. This phrase "the real world" is very misleading and subjective so ignore it.

Those who pretend to know what the real world is are full of you know what. Life is what you make of it, and you don't have to conform into the rat race if you don't want to. Leave it for the rodents, hence the term, "rat race".

45. There's Crime Every Week

Police send weekly emails of kids getting mugged on the street by thugs with multi-colored hair, attacked by unidentified men, or stabbed. It's amazing how it happens every week, yet the police are never able to find the perpetrators. Even Rutgers students commit crime as one pled guilty to cyber attacking the school. He and accomplices successfully shut down Rutgers's system, wonder why he decided to turn himself in. It was right before finals before Christmas so maybe he didn't want to upset Santa.

College avenue has frequent crime, and nothing is done about it. Go figure.

46. Scam Apartments Take Advantage of Students

I'm going to share with you a personal story about how an apartment scammed me using the Rutgers logo and how I lost time, money, and a semester. It caused me so much pain that it hurts to write this, but I have to, so you don't make the same mistake I did.

It was in the summer of 2017, I thought I could get a jump by taking summer courses at Rutgers and found an apartment named Rockoff Hall, owned by McKinney properties (funny how all the bad online reviews suddenly disappeared). They bore the Rutgers logo, so I assumed they were legit and somehow connected to the school. The

Rockoff manager told me they had only one room left and said it was private with no roommates, but there would be two other people in the other room.

These pics were found from the Rutgers
website

So I took it for the cheap price, however, when
I got there, someone was living in the "private"
room I was promised, and one of the guys in
the other room had a girlfriend living with
them. And I came to learn that this Dominican
guy was renting out unused beds in the
apartment to strangers. So I was in a very
tight situation. It was almost closing time and
knowing New Jersey tenant law, I just decided
to leave the next morning because I was told
that this was the only room left, and it was
impossible to sleep with all the noise from the

streets. I knew going to management would be pointless and didn't think they'd have any other accommodation based on the information they previously told me. By law, I had 24 hours to vacant, which I did, and was under no obligation to deal with them further after they failed to provide as promised. I also found out that they had recently cut their ties with the school and was no longer affiliated, yet still had the Rutgers "R" logo on their building, and their website/advertising presented themselves as if they still were connected.

New Jersey favors tenants, but these guys tried to screw me over. I requested my security deposit back, yet they said that I owed them rent even though I told them I left since they failed to provide the private room as promised. Still, they posted a court summons notice on the apartment door when they knew I wasn't living there, but thankfully, one of the other roommates told me the info.

Apparently, they were suing me for the summer rent amount which was over two thousand dollars. So, I showed up on the court date, surprising both the property manager and her lawyer, and after defending my position, they agreed to dismiss it. Later, I followed up requesting my security deposit to be returned and they never responded. So then, I decide to go to Rutgers's student legal department for assistance…read Reason # 92 to find out what happened next.

47. Registering for Classes Sucks

At any normal college, all you have to do to sign up for a class, is to log into your portal and select the classes you want and pay for it. Not the case with Rutgers. You have to jump through hoops just to get "approval" from admin and by the time it takes for them to do it, you lose your class, that is if they do it at all.

It's a dame five second task for them, yet they make you wait unnecessarily.

48. You have to Pay to Join a Club

You would think that after paying all that tuition money that the school could at least provide you clubs to join for free, but no, you must pay to participate in clubs. They usually cost between $30-50 dollars but it's a real pain, especially when you're a broke student. The school should cover it with the money they charge you.

And no, you're not going to make friends, nor will you learn anything. I'll give you an example, I went to martial arts club. First of all, I could only make the Sunday meetings, because the others were at night at different campuses and I couldn't drive there because I had no parking permit and I didn't want to take the bus because I'd end up arriving home past midnight. The instruction wasn't great either and I didn't really get better.

Stockton however, taught me much more. The jujitsu club had a real instructor who wore the traditional uniform and he taught us techniques that worked. The club size was just right, not too small, not to big, and I learned so much more compared to Rutgers and I can now hold my own should grappling become necessary.

49. No Time for Leisure

Unless your major is women's gender studies or some other useless subject, you're going to be so buried in books and schoolwork that you won't have any time to enjoy life. You'll become frustrated as you see other students uploading pictures of them traveling, partying, and having a good time while you toil away in the books. Have fun!

Yes, Rutgers has many clubs, but you won't have time to join them.

50. Super Liberal Campus

Everyone is pretty much Anti-Trump. I'm no die hard Trumpeteer, but the politics is ridiculous. Everything is leftwing – pro LGBT, pro transgender, pro liberal, pro socialism, pro illegal immigration, and pro feminism while being anti-God, anti-religion, anti-nuclear family, anti-male, anti-white, and anti-heterosexual. It is a very spoiled and entitled campus filled with the dumbest student body that I had ever seen. I don't care if they get good grades, that doesn't mean anything these days.

Academics proves nothing, just have a casual conversation with these students and you'll see how "bright" they really are. It's almost as if it's like a cult where everyone automatically assumes you're a pro-Bernie supporter and in favor of socialism over capitalism. I read an article about how one student described his experience of wearing a Trump hat on campus at Rutgers and how students aggressively reacted with some even confronting him.

Academia thinks they can create a world of order because they're so "sophisticated". One day, my molecular genetics professor handed out our exams in piles of alphabetical order. The 165 students crowded in and made a mess as any common man would have predicted, but the professor got upset stating he didn't understand why crowds act so irrational. This is why most scientists never achieve great success in the real world, because they don't understand human behavior since they're too left brained and analytical. They fail to realize that we're still mammals with the same basic instincts and urges. Academics think they can shape the world into their orderly utopia, but can't grasp that nature has its own balance, its own systematic chaos, and that it is foolish to try to control it but wise to work with it. This is what ancients knew long ago but who cares, they're were all primitives according to the "brilliant" professors of Rutgers. That's why guys like Donald Trump succeed and professors teach, because street smarts beat book smarts.

If Rutgers is this bad, I can only imagine what it's like at Ivy League schools but thank God I didn't go there. It has been my greatest displeasure attending Rutgers and I hope no normal person should ever have to go there and suffer like I did.

51. False Rape Culture

Men are attacked and blamed for everything so if you're a regular guy with a normal amount of testosterone, you're going to find yourself in a tight predicament.

52. You Can't Do Real Research

It's all about identifying protein structures for Big Pharma or materials science for the military, that's what are acceptable research areas at this school and pretty much at most big-name state universities. I wanted to do research in longevity to use herbal combinations to extend life, but that wasn't good enough for Rutgers. What a surprise.

53. Cocky City Dwellers

They wear suits, they wear skirts, and they look down at you the struggling student. They expect you to treat them as if they are superior to you because they make more money. These people have an attitude and it'll make you want to punch their lights out to bring them back down to earth.

54. Street Bums

They're everywhere and they'll ask you for money. While waiting for the bus at George Street, a homeless guy asked me for twenty dollars because he was hungry. Later, another asked for a dollar because he said he had "no food at his house". You have a house, I thought? Well, that makes you richer than me because I can't even afford one. Yes, it's a problem the government refuses to address and being in the city, you'll see them everywhere.

55. STDs are Everywhere

Rutgers students do some crazy s**t. I don't know if it's the drugs, the parties, sex with random strangers, or all of the above, but they are not the kind that you want to take home.

56. Dirty Dorms

Paying top dollar, you'd expect the living quarters to be decent but no, you'll be living in ghetto style rooms. Even if you're in the Honor's Program, it still sucks. The "perks" are not worth doing the extra work. Good luck trying to get any sleep with all the parties. I knew a girl who got a seizure after her first semester there due to her roommates partying and smoking marijuana. My calculus professor shared with the class the roommates he had on campus – the first roommate got arrested, the second roommate was a drug dealer, and the third roommate was an even bigger drug dealer.

Today, this man is a bald underpaid professor teaching math and working four different jobs and gets up at 4 A.M. everyday…awesome.

57. Rutgers Hides Millions in Offshore Bank Accounts

I remember seeing the report that came out where over a hundred colleges were caught hiding billions collectively in offshore bank accounts. They do this to avoid paying taxes, and the amount of money these schools are hoarding in foreign tax havens is over 500 billion. Yes, you read right.

Rutgers was among one of the schools on the list, yet they still pretend like they're poor. They use this excuse to keep hiking up costs and delivering fourth-rate education to students. What a bunch of crooks and liars.

58. Campus is Too Big

They've grown bigger than they can manage. Many of the buildings that are for science labs and other courses look like houses because the school keeps buying property. It has become very confusing and chaotic for students, and it seems like no one knows what's going on anymore. Like I said, it functions like a third-world country where organized chaos reigns supreme.

Travel time to get to class is unnecessary long and hectic, yet admin doesn't care. They are just collecting money and could give a dame about students.

59. Really Bad Tutors Who Don't Give a S**t

Many are foreign and so are difficult to understand as their English isn't good. I don't know why admin gives them these jobs, but most of the tutors don't care just like professors. Unless you're a hot babe, you're out of luck. Usually there's only one tutor and there are so many students who come in for help. Group sessions are worthless, because there's just too many people and thus goofing around is common. You won't learn anything.

Mass produced education is not working.

Notes and Tutors is a startup that offers tutoring services to students, but they are equally bad, as is hiring former professors. It's very expensive and you don't get the help you need because these guys can't teach themselves and there's just not enough time to learn the material.

The internet is your best teacher.

60. Girls get Special Treatment

Babes get it all - personalized extra help at tutoring centers, personal attention in labs, and preference from professors. Whenever you have attractive females, professors, tutors, and admin drool all over to help them thinking that they'll get lucky. Yes, it's sad and pathetic, and it's unfair for guys who really need help.

61. Classes are a Big Waste of Time

Everyone is goofing off on Facebook, there's no order, and with so many disturbing private conversations going on, you can't hear what the professor is saying. Classes are packed, disconnecting you from professors which makes you not care anymore.

I've met multiple students who were tutors confess to me that they never went to class for courses like chemistry, because they weren't learning anything. So, they just taught themselves and ended up getting an A.

71

Many seasoned students do this because going to class really is a waste of time.

62. Cheating is Mandatory for Survival

If you're a STEM major, there's no way you're going to learn everything unless you're Brainiac, so most of your time going is spent looking up answers online. I met a math tutor who told me he cheated in chemistry, and I've seen other students cheat in class. Everybody cheats, and I don't blame them because why should you, a young person in your prime years, drive yourself crazy memorizing crap that you're never going to use? This is the time when you are supposed to be happy, exploring, and enjoying life, not suffering by doing meaningless nonsense. Professors don't teach but rather read off PowerPoint slides and then run home.

Cheat, who cares. Just get the right answers by any means necessary and get the good grades, get out, and make money.

63. Rigged Reputation

Thanks to federal funding and connections with the industrial/academia complex, Rutgers and other big state schools, continue to reap the benefits of having a reputable name. However, this is misleading because they're 250 years old. They're living off an outdated reputation, and while it may have been great 100 years ago, today it is nothing but a dark shadow of its former self. I remember my calculus professor there told the class that Rutgers has one of the best math programs in the nation. Snickers and laughs were heard in the classroom, because even students knew it was just a bunch of crap. That may have been the case when Rutgers was at its prime, but not today. If it is, then American education has truly fallen to a new low.

I suggest talking to alumni and real people for an unbiased view. Go on the state government's website to really investigate what the student success rates really are and if most graduates are really getting the super cool high paying jobs as being advertised. You'll find out just as I did, that this is false. The problem is too many people believe the hype, but the reality is only a fraction of its entire student body achieves the super success that you see being advertised. Don't fall for it!

64. Labs are Taught by Grad <u>Students,</u> NOT Professors

When I took physics, I never saw my professor. It was taught by a Chinese grad student who couldn't teach nor speak English well and there was another Chinese girl who was his assistant. He once sent the class an email that if we didn't get the next lab quiz right, he would "punish" us. This is the problem of letting in all these foreign students, their culture isn't the same and ultimately the American student suffers! The professor was never in class. For all I knew, he could have been sleeping, drinking, partying at clubs, or reclining at the beach in Hawaii.

How can a school do this, what is the point of having a professor whom you never see?

65. It's a Soulless Place

Spirit is virtually none existent on campus; you feel like a mechanical subhuman. You're just a number, a fish in an ocean, and nobody is there is help you. Psychological therapy is common among students, even among A-students. Oh yes, I've met them along with witnessing many other surprises as you're probably discovering yourself through this book.

66. Political Correctness

You must keep your tongue on a leash and be careful of what you say, because the goon squad is ready to slap you with charges of racism, discrimination, and bigotry. That's what you get when you go to an ultra-liberal university. That's why Rutgers is voted the number one "Dump Trump" school in America.

67. Hub for Migrants

New Jersey went from a Garden State to a Garbage State thanks to mass illegal immigration. Things aren't going to get better as Governor Murphy stated he wants to turn NJ into a 'sanctuary state'. Rutgers is flooded with illegal aliens and no sanitary measures have been taken. When you get on the shuttle bus, you can see it. These people carry diseases and letting them ride free on the bus puts students at risk for catching tuberculosis, bed bugs, and other diseases that were once wiped out of America. This has also taken the resources and opportunities away from American citizens as now immigrants are being favored over them.

Minorities get preference and this unfair treatment discriminates Americans whether them being Caucasian or Asian.

68. Too Many Immigrants

A lot of them bring their dirty filthy ways and habits imported from a third world s**t-hole where corruption, lying, and cheating are normal. They speak in their native language in public, are loud and ill-mannered, and have no courtesy for others as if they're living in their own country. This is what happens when you let too many races in, they start to take over and run it like it's their place. They don't assimilate to the American culture and this leads to clashing of multiple ethnic living standards. Rutgers feels more like subset culture of third world diversity, it doesn't feel like you're in America.

Ask any honest Asian American, and they'll tell you about those "Off The Boat Asians" who bring their communist ways and it gets really annoying. The same is also true for Indian and Hispanic immigrant students who come to American universities and act like it's their country. The problem is too many immigrants from third world countries are being allowed in America and as a result, American schools are flooded with entitled students who demand all citizen benefits while the American student is given the middle finger.

Be prepared, because you'll be in for a cultural shock.

69. Rigged Admissions

Too many students are there not based on grades but because they can throw a football or dribble a basketball. It's dumbing down the school, and kids who are there to learn are being forced to deal with stupid people.

On a side note, too many professors are there not because they can teach, but because they're Black, Muslim, or liberal. That's how colleges screen these days for hiring professors. So long as they're anything but traditional, they're qualified. Being a progressive, socialist/communist, and anti-God is preferred.

Americans who speak clear English need not apply. Don't believe me? Go to class and see if you learn anything.

70. It's High School Part 2

Students behave like they're still in high school. In my chemistry class, there was a Black kid who would hop around, and kept making silly comments in a squeaky voice to the professor. His behavior was that of a high school delinquent. Sure, it may be funny for some, but for many it was distracting especially when you've got over a hundred students all trying to pass a difficult class like chemistry.

One day, this Black kid stood up on the professor's desk and sang some metrosexual song in front of the class.

The maturity level at this university is that of kindergarten. Grade school kids are more civilized. Some professors are very unprofessional like my calculus one who kept cracking jokes and checking the scores for his favorite sports team. In other classes, students were goofing off and/or having their own conversations since the classrooms are so large.

Nobody seems to care, nobody says anything, and professors don't bother either because if they try to establish some order, a lawsuit is right around the corner for racism, discrimination, and anything else the brigade of scumbag weasel lawyers can think of. So, professors just read their slides off their Power Point and run home.

71. Stupid Sign Holders, Religious Nuts, and Preachers

On my way to class, I saw a guy holding some stupid sign about how Jesus is the only way.

How original. Stunts like these are really getting old but can be frequently seen on campus. Everyone is trying to sell you something to believe in, and all you've got to do is give them money and watch all your sins disappear!

72. They Allow People on Campus Who Shouldn't be there

Once, while leaving class, some random Black guy who looked like a bum gave out his hand to which I hesitantly shook, and he asked if I wanted to buy some candy. There were others with him, but these Black guys were obviously not students and were just there to sell some candy for whatever charity they were part of. It gets really annoying, but you can't say anything or else you're called a racist.

Students don't want to shake hands with random strangers and deal with salesmen trying to get them sold on some stupid product or charity. Why doesn't the school clean these bums off the campus? Liberalism, that's why, and you're paying for it, sucker.

73. Dating Scene Sucks

Primarily because you have no time since you're studying 24/7. Besides, thanks to social media, most girls there are entitled, spoiled, overprivileged, and just flat out crazy. Guys are looking for one thing and the male thirst for sex never ceases. Girls act like sluts and guys act like dogs, welcome to college dating.

You're better off working to make money, and then get yourself a nice body, a nice car, and dressy clothes. Then drive around campus and honk whenever you see a girl that you fancy and watch as she comes running over eager to offer anything from sex to back massages just to be a part of your luxurious life. Yes, society is pathetic, and yes college dating sucks. The alternative is to just build bulging muscles, and then walk around campus shirtless. If you're a girl, get fit and show off some skin, it never fails to lure in hungry hounds who will pay for all your expenses.

74. Loneliness

Despite the number of students, I never felt more alone. Normally I enjoy solitude, but the combination of Rutgers and city living has a way of making you feel like a loser if you don't have friends and this is coming from someone who is naturally a loner.

Unless you've got an easy major in social sciences or gender studies, there's no time for that. You'll have no time to do anything unless you've got an easy major with a light workload. There's no time to join clubs, "get involved on campus", or any of the BS colleges sell you.

75. Social Justice Warriors are Running the Place

Recently, they had Joe Biden to lecture men about sex violence only to take selfies with them later.

Former Vice President Joe Biden poses with
Rutgers students for a group selfie.
Photo: Nick Romanenko, Rutgers University

Not to mention, Biden has a history of creepily
groping women of all ages.

U.S. Secretary of Defense, Ash Carter,
delivers his acceptance speech at the White
House in Washington on Feb. 17, 2015.
Gary Cameron—Reuters

That's how your tuition is being spent, sucker!
This is the corrupt political juggernaut you're
entering. If you are traditional, or anything but
a socialist, you're going to be alone in a
cesspit of darkness.

76. Women Blame Men for "Toxic Masculinity"

Francesca Petrucci, aka, the "Annoying Vegan", wrote an article on The Daily Targum, Rutgers's newspaper, blaming the Florida shooting was due to toxic masculinity. She mentioned Elliot Rodgers as an example, using his quote, "Tomorrow is the day of retribution, the day in which I will have my revenge," he says in what he calls his last video. "You girls have never been attracted to me. I don't know why you girls aren't attracted to me, but I will punish you all for it." He specifically criticized sorority members.

Rodgers also said beforehand, "On the day of retribution I'm going to enter the hottest sorority house of UCSB," he said in the video. "I'll take great pleasure in slaughtering all of you."

As you can see from such statements, these kinds of despicable acts were not committed by testosterone laden man, but by weak insecure mentally ill boy who did not know how to handle himself. The manly man is happy and healthy while the miserable one despises him and seeks to steal his joy. Rodgers claimed that men are the majority who commit such massacres using poorly researched sources while indirectly saying that men are the blame. The truth is that nearly 100% of these shooters were on dangerous medication like Ritalin, Prozac, and even marijuana. The whack job psychologists who deal these drugs out like candy are the ones responsible for creating this new breed of mentally ill sheeple.

Instead of debating about it, an analysis can be done measuring the brain patterns and T-levels of those in mental institutes and in prison for various crimes, compared to those living normal healthy lives. You won't find a definitive difference, because there are those who achieve great financial and professional success and those who commit atrocious crimes due to high testosterone. The hormone is not to blame, it is the misused aggression and mental problems of the perpetrators.

High testosterone is not necessarily found in these criminals, but severe brain abnormalities resulting from drug addiction, pornography, and negative environment factors are. These people needed mental help, not hormone therapy. Still, students like Francesca, don't understand this and believe in silly things like apps that claim to reduce rape, and the estrogen-laced subjective scientists at Rutgers concur.

77. The President of the School DOES NOT Want to Lower Tuition

Rutgers was quick to support Phil Murphy, but when he became governor and announced his hopes to lower college tuition, the president of Rutgers said to hold his horses. You see folks, it's always all about the money. The president listed a whole bunch of BS excuses against lowering tuition, but if the school believed so blindly in Murphy while knowing about his intentions for lowering costs, then why did they show so much support?

Like many colleges, Rutgers is just in it for the money and purposely vote for democrats because they usually give them the most funding, but Murphy in this case threw a curve ball. Eventually, their socialist ways will backfire and what you're seeing here is just the beginning.

78. Transferring Courses are a Pain

Ask any student and they will attest to the unnecessarily harshness of Rutgers regarding the transfer of classes. For me, I wanted to transfer organic chemistry, but Rutgers said I couldn't unless I took organic chemistry 2 at the same institution. I was struggling on funds and so I asked if I could take it at community college, but they said no, and to either take it at my previous school or retake organic chemistry 1 there and then take the second semester too.

These are the odd silly rules their school has, and the problem is each department has their own rules. The math department may accept a course, but the engineering department won't approve, so you'll have to swing through hoops when you otherwise shouldn't have to.

79. Student Success is Exaggerated

Don't let the job "statistics" fool you, employment rates are not great for graduates. Sure, they may get jobs like everyone else, but these are positions that they could have gotten without a degree. I've seen a biology graduate working at a residential building, and other students who just ended up working at typical positions that they didn't need a degree to begin with.

80. Dominated by Big Pharma

The pharmaceutical industry is big in Jersey and so they love students to major in chemistry, biotechnology, and of course medicine to join them in their quest to make the world hooked on drugs. If you prefer a more holistic approach, you'll be laughed at by the academics who will call your vitamins pseudoscience even though two-time Nobel prize winner Linus Pauling was a pioneer in the field among others.

81. Student Protests

It's amazing how the government lets these idiots block traffic preventing people from getting to work to provide for their families. Businesses suffer, citizens can't continue with their day, and many other complications occur all because of a bunch of snowflake fools with overinflated egos who want to stop everything just so everyone can listen to them shout their rubbish on a microphone. They're violent and therefore, dangerous.

My advice - if you ever see them while driving, just put the pedal to the medal and get out of there! If questioned, tell the police that you feared your life was in danger.

82. Professors Like Failing You

There are professors, especially in the life sciences department, who purposely believe it is their job to fail 1/3 or even 1/2 of the class in order to "weed out" the weak links. Not good for you the American student. This is what happens when you bring in foreign academics from third-world nations.

I was surprised to meet Indian and Asian students who told me that they had to repeat courses because they failed previously due to horrible professors. It's not uncommon to hear of students retaking classes for the second, third, or even fourth time. That's how bad it is over there, and the problem is these professors are untouchable in their tenured positions.

83. Their Facilities are a Joke

They like to advertise their "world class" education but the reality is, you're never going to get anywhere near the cool equipment unless you're a grad student. That's just how it goes, so don't go in thinking you're going to invent the cure for cancer or something because you're not. It's all slick marketing and the sooner you realize it, the sooner you can save yourself the disappointment.

84. Not Respected

Rutgers used to have a good name, but now it's viewed as a garbage school. I knew an all-star high school student who was dubbed a genius and he told me in his honor classes, Rutgers is seen by students as a joke. You want to get out of New Jersey, this state is a total s**t-hole anyway.

85. The Weekend Bus Schedule Sucks

Campus is dead on the weekends and what's worse is that professors normally schedule tests on these days, Sunday being a favorite. The problem, however, is that the bus system is terrible on weekends, so you are dependent on about two or maybe three shuttles which have very confusing long routes.

For example, if you want to go to Cook campus, you will usually end up having no choice but to board the bus that goes to Busch or Livingston which is the opposite way of Cook because as previously stated, there's only about two buses available during weekends and they have to abide by a long route that takes them all across the multiple campuses of Rutgers.

Yes, it's retarded and very annoying. The app is never accurate and if you miss the bus, you're most definitely going to be waiting for an hour minimum. If your stop is on or anywhere near George Street, good luck, you'll need it.

86. Libraries are Packed

Whenever I went to the library to study with others, it was always a pain to find an open table or any spot for that matter, where you can sit and study in peace and quiet. Like I said before, this school is too dame big for its own good. Getting to the library is a trip in itself, and once you get there, you're too worn out to study, that is if you can find a spot. Book availability is surprisingly limited to antiques as most of the texts are written over a hundred years ago, so they provide very little help in your academic pursuits.

It matters little which campus you go to – Busch, Livingston, Cook, the facilities are nothing special and they're always packed.

87. Subpar Education

Contrary to what you might think, Rutgers education IS NOT better than any other schooling you may have received. As I stated before, I've met plenty of electrical engineering majors who were about to graduate tell me that they had no idea what they're doing and did not feel confident about entering the work force.

Many students hate Rutgers classes, many students have told me that they hate Rutgers itself, and many have admitted that they wished they took the prerequisite and basic requirement classes at community college.

You will be wasting your time and money attending there. There is nothing "rigorous" or "world class" about it. It's just dumping tons of department approved coursework in the guise of making the program "more competitive" with other schools.

Save your money and sanity, don't go to this s**t-hole.

Bigger is not better. Less is more.

88. Online Homework

Building off that, the biggest annoyance Rutgers gives to students is massive amounts of online homework. WebAssign sucks, just ask any student.

Dumping tons of online homework and quizzes does not make students better. It just drives them crazy spending hours and hours in front of the computer clicking on a mouse trying to solve ridiculous problems that doesn't even prepare them well for tests.

Quantity does not equate to quality, but Rutgers doesn't care. Online work saves them money while still charging you top dollar. Don't believe me? Go enroll and you'll see for yourself. Don't come crying to me afterwards.

89. Lack of Class Availability

Registering for courses is unnecessarily difficult, but the other problem many students face, is the lack of availability because Rutgers is understaffed for its size and many students suffer by missing classes which delays their graduation. Many students get the "RU Screw", because they couldn't get the courses they needed thus failing to graduate on time.

90. Cafeteria

If you live on campus, good luck getting grub at a reasonable time. Whenever I passed by the freshman cafeteria, I was always in shock because the line was always so long that it went out of the entrance. You will be waiting an hour just to get in.

91. Electronic Participation Devices

Rutgers first introduced me to the handheld remote controllers to participate in classroom exercises. I had never heard of nor used one before until coming to Rutgers and I hated it. It was just another unnecessary expense that's overly priced, and I learned nothing from the in-class exercises. Students have no idea what the questions are and end up randomly selecting answers or copying others.

92. Student Legal Services

Continuing off of how Rockoff Hall screwed me over, I went to Rutgers's student legal services office and met the director who gave me the contact of a lawyer he recommended, so I spoke with him and paid $35 for him to write a letter to Rockoff demanding the owed security deposit of $300. Rockoff took nearly a year to respond and after the lawyer reached out to them multiple times, they finally sent a check for the security deposit amount of $300, but there was one problem…the check bounced.

I told the lawyer, and after many attempts to reach Rockoff's legal team, he advised to file a complaint and represent myself because his hourly rate would exceed the amount I would be suing for. Great, so I wasted $35, and now I'm on my own, thank you Rutgers.

By NJ law, Rockoff owed me double the security deposit for their negligence, but I'm a student, so I don't have time to sue, go to court, and run back and forth. Later after I left Rutgers, I went to the police in my county and the officer was nice enough to call them on my behalf. What we found out was that Rockoff Hall, then owned by McKinney Properties, was bought by Greystar and renamed to SoCam 209.

The officer got the contact for McKinney's higher up manager, and I followed up with him as instructed. This guy said due to the transfer of ownership, McKinney was no longer responsible and gave me the contact Greystar's regional manager. So, I contacted her and while she said they would work to get the resolved, I never heard back from her despite several emails and leaving a message on her cellphone.

So, I thought about suing but the problem was I had to go back to the s**t-hole city of New Brunswick because if I wanted to sue them, I had to do it in the same county where the property was located.

New Jersey law favors the tenant, huh? Bulls**t!

2019 Update – I sued Rockoff Hall Urban Renewal LLC and got my money back.

93. Bad Food

Despite the great size of Rutgers, there isn't much variety regarding on campus eating, because the food selections really come down to the same typical choices that you find at every college campus – Asian food, pizza, burgers & fries, and other junk.

The one place I liked was a Chipotle imitation place on the Livingston campus. There was one Middle Eastern place on College Ave, but I wouldn't recommend it. I've never been inside the café for those who live on campus, mainly due to the long lines that I mentioned before but can only assume it'll be just typical college food.

Honestly, for the prices they charge you, you're better off shopping at the grocery and cooking at home. Or, you can do the right thing and ditch this school altogether and save your money on overpriced garbage food.

94. Rude Bus Drivers

There was one Russian guy who yelled at me and another girl for apparently blocking his view when we moved aside to let some students depart at their stop. A Latina driver kept calling me a boy whenever I asked for information, and there was one Black woman who happily let Black bums on board for free rides but refused a white guy who didn't necessarily look like a bum. She also let on other shady looking Black people and even when it was jam packed, she didn't give people enough time to depart at stops. Some students like me, got stuck between the door due to this and had to yell at her to reopen it so we could leave.

Welcome to Rutgers, the s**t-hole state university of New Jersey!

95. Silly City and School Events

During the school year, there were frequent ridiculous school events like the false rape nonsense where the creep himself Joe Biden visited to blast men for being rapists even though he himself likes touching other people's wives and daughters. Additionally, the s**t-hole city of New Brunswick had their own events to please bureaucrats. The only good thing about was they swept off the bums for the day, the bad thing was due to these events, roads were closed off forcing you to go around a different route which easily quadrupled your commute time.

Don't forget, you're paying to deal with this crap.

96. Unpleasant Atmosphere

Walking anywhere takes 30 minutes minimum and when you do that, you realize that you're living in a jungle. Honking, crazy people, and so many other random noises will fill your eardrums. You'll be craving to get away into nature as the only things you'll see are tall beaten up buildings, dirty buses, bums, elitists, cocky suits and skirts, and snobby students.

97. Nobody Knows What They're Doing

Once you've spoken with advisers, professors, and other administrators, you'll realize what many seasoned students already know and that is that nobody knows what the hell they're doing. Deans will say one thing while professors say another. One advisor will tell you to go on one course path while another will say differently. You will quickly learn that nobody knows what they're talking about and it gets very annoying, and yes, very frustrating.

98. You See the Same People

Once you get into the routine of your classes, you end up seeing the same people repeatedly because you will be taking the same route to get to your destination and so will everyone else with similar schedules. So, don't believe the lie that you'll broaden your horizons and meet a lot of people. The reality is that you'll be dealing with the same faces in your classes and program. Yes, clubs and social groups help, but it gets very redundant very easily and very quickly.

99. Really Old Campus Buildings

Classmates have told me that they were initially confused because the lab and other science buildings look like small houses. Like I said, the school is ancient, it's over 200 years old. If you go to any of the campuses, most of the buildings were indeed houses at one time but Rutgers bought them out. The only campus that has some new structures is Livingston, but the others are relics.

Bathrooms reek of a bad stench, and rooms are nothing special to look at. It's you're call, but I'd prefer to go to a more modernized university like Stockton, who just opened several brand new sleek looking buildings. And they also upgraded all their other facilities. It's neat, clean, pleasant, and nestled in a natural peaceful setting.

100. Elitism

I already mentioned the arrogant suits and skirts, and professors who walk around the dirty streets of New Brunswick. However, on campus, you see the same mentality. There is clearly a division among students where there are those who think they're above everyone else and look down on others. The same can be seen in academia and administration who think too highly of themselves. It's not any different than what you'd expect at an Ivy League school.

I'm not saying there's anything wrong with it, just pointing out to you that Rutgers is not the friendly welcoming place that they portray themselves to be. I remember walking to the bus stop and to my surprise saw my calculus professor walking to the bagel shop. He clearly saw me, yet kept walking with his head held high, no hello or anything, just a complete snob. I had previously asked for help and he just ignored me. Careful kids, this is what you'll be getting yourselves into.

101. Rutgers Might Shut Down

I remember seeing the sharks from the popular show, Shark Tank, giving advice to future students about making sure that their college's financial track record checks out okay before deciding to enroll. I found that very interesting that they would suggest such a thing. Some also said that formal education may not even be necessary at all. It's not only rich businessmen who are saying this. One professor from the Harvard Business School, predicts that half of American universities will go bankrupt in the next 10-45 years. We already know Rutgers is hoarding money like many other schools in offshore bank accounts that they keep hidden from the public. Why would they be doing that, could it be they're preparing for the worst?

Based on their actions, I would not put too much faith in them especially with their monkey management. It is very possible that they, along with many other schools, could go bankrupt. They just recently increased the minimum wage for student workers and are essentially dependent on government funding while their education continues to get worse. So, I'm suspecting that top admins are already storing cash offshore to plan for their escape when the whole thing comes crashing down.

Only time will tell, but don't be surprised to see Rutgers and many other schools go bankrupt and shut down, because I won't be.

Donald Trump is not likely to bail them out either.

The Verdict: THIS SCHOOL SUCKS!

Its official, Rutgers is a s**t-hole university. They should shut it down and refund every student who has not achieved as they were promised to. Colleges need to be responsible for the debt and financial sacrifice students make, but this is not going to happen because of the government/academia complex. You've heard of Big Government and perhaps Big Pharma, well now you've got Big Education, a corrupt branch of greedy administrators who have ties to bureaucrats who approve legislation to funnel money to their school in exchange for favors.

It's all politics, and it reeks of corruption.

Better Alternatives to Stinky Rutgers and Yes, I Hope this Lowers their Enrollment

Transfer to smaller NJ schools like Stockton, Monmouth, and Montclair, or try other states like Pennsylvania or Florida if you prefer leaving New Jersey. Rutgers is just going to hike up your anxiety levels and thoughts of suicide will be knocking at your door. More and more community colleges like Ocean

County College, are offering bachelor's degrees where you can complete all of your coursework at the community college campus. Don't fall for "the college experience" sales pitch. The college experience can be summed up in three bullet points –

- Parties
- Sex
- Drugs, alcohol, and pot

Not to mention the annoying rules you'll have to follow like fire drills (as though you were in high school) and the big expense.
Roommates are a hit or miss, but from what I heard, they're mostly a miss.

Ultimately, it's you who must make the choice that's best for you, but I personally prefer smaller schools that are in the suburbs with a more natural environment where you can actually park on campus and walk to where you need to go.

Save yourself from Getting Screwed

Avoid this dump at all costs. If you neglect these words and go, well good luck, but don't come crying to me if things go bad. Rutgers may have been great 100 years ago, but now, you're better off going to a community college. This institution has become a third world s**t-hole, and if you don't believe me, you can read the many students' reviews on the Students Review website. If you get into Rutgers and have a free ride offer, or are in graduate school, fine, but proceed with caution. If you are in any way paying for tuition, I strongly advise you to seek another school. Rutgers is overhyped, overrated, and overpriced.

Spend your money elsewhere, else your education will suffer. If you're going as a grad student, okay, it won't be as bad as an undergraduate, but you will still suffer. Even if this book becomes a bestseller and it reaches the bureaucrats at Rutgers, they still won't do anything to improve the education. They'll probably just laugh in their arrogance while counting student money.

Student's Review Reveals All

Here's what other students have said about Rutgers –

"I hate this university so much. Shitty professors who don't give a damn about you."

"I was a physics major and the program was absolutely awful, and I think I would sue them to the ground if they were a legit private institution that could be addressed in such a manner."

"I hated Rutgers University and I'm glad I'm transferring out. Campus is disgusting, you cannot walk to any of the different divisions in the campus without taking a damn bus. it's empty on the weekends. Some of the professors stink balls, especially if you choose to do life sciences. Arrogant professors in the general biology and gen chem department. For some reason, they like to fail 1/3 / 1/2 of the class."

To read more real student reviews of Rutgers, visit the Students Review website which is not censored like other sites such as Rate My Professor.

Where I am now?

For those curious about what I'm doing now, I'm back at my old school, Stockton University and couldn't be happier. Stockton is going up and up, and from what I have heard, is now a big competitor. Students are now choosing between Stockton or Rutgers, and more and more are choosing to have beachfront education at Stockton's new campus at Atlantic City over dirty city stupidity at Rutgers.

I love the small class sizes and personal one on one quality education I get from professors. I'm actually learning there and doing research whereas at Rutgers, it was just brutal survival.

How I Did at other Schools

I took the same classes at Stockton and at community college and GOT STELLAR GRADES. For example, at Rutgers I flunked chem 2, at community college I got an A, and it wasn't a walk in the park either, but the professor was good, and the atmosphere was appropriate for learning, not a zoo like Rutgers. This is a common theme you'll hear from those who abandoned Rutgers and pursued their education elsewhere.

So join the party and say hello to better quality education!

RU Student? My Frank Advice to You

Get out. Do it now before it's too late. No, you are not going to move to New York City and become rich and successful. I know those who have, and you won't do it unless you're willing to suck some serious d**k and kiss a lot of corporate a$$. Also, joining secret societies like Free Masonry helps too. Yes, they're real, and yes, they're everywhere. I heard the rumors, but after meeting one and learning about how they occupy even mediocre positions that you wouldn't expect, it is now clear that the game is rigged.

Don't go to Rutgers, you have been warned.

2019 Update

This Spring, I finished my bachelor's degree in biology with concentrations in biotechnology and neurobiology at Stockton University. I did well in courses such as calculus, calculus 2, general physics 1 & 2, molecular genetics, and more. It took me a while to recover from the horrendous experience at Rutgers, but I made it and I'm doing better. I also got into medical school and now thinking about prospects. So you see, you can succeed without going to this dumpster school called Rutgers. I have met others who also left Rutgers and have done well for themselves, so you don't have to buy into the herd mentality that Rutgers is the only way to go.

One of my chemistry professors told the class that her daughter was completing her bachelor's degree at Kean at Ocean County College (Ocean County Community College and Kean University have an agreement that allows students to earn a bachelor's degree from Kean at the Ocean County campus), because it's cheaper and convenient. She explained that everyone thinks that they need to go to these big state schools, but they are overspending when they can get the same, if not better, education at a smaller school. There are also several advantages you get such as -

- Smaller class sizes
- More availability of facilities due to less people
- Personal help from professors
- One on one tutoring
- Better relationships since it's a close setting
- A more supportive community
- Affordability
- Closer to home so works great for those with a job

These advantages continue to grow as more people are waking up to the fallacies of big universities. What you have just read about Rutgers is typical at pretty much every state school. They're overcrowded, maintain a roster of professors with poor teaching ability, and generally are not good at helping you because they're too big for their own good.

There's also another important variable you should be aware of -

FREE College!

In case you haven't heard, community colleges in the state of New Jersey are free as recently made by Governor Murphy. That's right, so why would you want to pay top dollar when you can get a good education at your local college for free? This trend is likely to spread across other states, and even if it isn't, community college is much cheaper and offers smooth transfers to four-year universities thanks to agreements made between colleges

Unless you're getting an all expense free ride, I would strongly recommend avoiding Rutgers. If you live close by and already have a strong academic background from high school, fine, go ahead, but if you are like me and not an academic nerd, beware of Rutgers. Regardless, Rutgers should be avoided because you would save so much time, money, and headache by going to community college for two years. Then you can later decide where you want to go.

What if You Have to Go to Rutgers?

Some of you may need to go because you have no other option. At the very least, if you really want to or have to go to Rutgers, my suggestion would be to take your first two years at community college and then transfer. This will make your experience there much less hectic, because at Rutgers, you're going to have around 500 students or more in your perquisite classes, and you'll most likely have a rough time unless you already know the subject material. Courses like calculus, accounting, physics, biology, and chemistry are better done at community college.

Get your prerequisite requirements done at community college and then transfer. That way, all you'll have left are just two years of taking the upper level classes which won't be as bad. Classes are smaller and it's more of specialization courses towards your major which are less stressful. Commute if you can to save money, otherwise all the best. If you are thinking about going to Rutgers for graduate school, fine, assuming you have the finances. Your time will be much less stressful compared to your undergrad counterparts.

Good Luck with Your Education!

Many thanks for reading this short book, and I hope it was enough for you to avoid this joke of an academic institution. I know how hard the struggle is these days for kids.

I wish you the best of luck with your education and success!

If you liked this book and would like to learn more about the reality of college and my recommendations for aspiring students, get my book, *COLLEGE EXPOSED*.

Sincerely,

G.S. Luthra, MBA, BFA, BA, BS (all not from Rutgers)

www.gsluthracreations.com

CPSIA information can be obtained
at www.ICGtesting.com
Printed in the USA
LVHW041312030621
689239LV00004B/308